CANDACE PARKER

"Power, Purpose, and the Making of a Legend"

By
Thorne Mavick

Copyright © 2025 Thorne Mavick

All rights reserved.

No part of this book may be reproduced, stored in a retrieval system, or transmitted in any form or by any means—electronic, mechanical, photocopying, recording, or otherwise—without prior written permission from the author, except for brief quotations used in reviews or articles.

This is a work of nonfiction. All efforts have been made to ensure accuracy and fairness. Any errors or omissions are unintentional.

Published by Thorne Mavick

Printed in the United States of America

Epigraph

"She didn't just change the game. She changed the story of what a woman could be when she chose her truth over their expectations."
— *Unknown*

Contents

Acknowledgements iv

Introduction 1

Chapter 1: The Early Years – From St. Louis to Stardom 5

Chapter 2: The College Years – Tennessee & Pat Summitt 10

Chapter 3: Entering the WNBA – A New Era Begins .. 15

Chapter 4: Breaking Barriers – Personal and Professional Struggles 20

Chapter 5: The Champion's Mindset – Mental Toughness and Resilience 25

Chapter 6: The Glory Years – Rising to Prominence ... 30

Chapter 7: The Sky's the Limit – A New Chapter in Chicago 35

Chapter 8: A Champion's Journey – Challenges Beyond the Court 40

Chapter 9: The Final Stretch – Navigating Retirement 45

Chapter 10: Impact on the WNBA – Elevating Women's Sports 50

Chapter 11: Personal Life – Love, Loss, and the Balance of It All 55

Conclusion – The Lasting Legacy of Candace Parker .. 65

Acknowledgements

This book is an independent biography of Candace Parker, compiled through careful research and analysis of various publicly available resources, interviews, and publications about her life and career. It is not written by Candace Parker herself, nor has it been endorsed or authorized by her.

The information presented within these pages has been gathered from multiple sources, including interviews, articles, books, and public appearances made by Candace Parker and other media outlets that have shared insights into her life, work, and impact. Every effort has been made to ensure the accuracy and reliability of the content; however, as with any work of biography, interpretations and perspectives may vary.

All trademarks, brand names, and other proprietary identifiers related to Candace Parker, the WNBA, or any of her business ventures remain the property of their respective owners. This book is a tribute to her legacy and a reflection on her significant impact on the world of basketball and beyond, but it is not an official or authorized account of her life.

The author and publisher do not intend to infringe upon any copyrights or trademarks and have made every effort to provide proper attribution for all quoted or referenced material.

Page Blank Intentionally

Introduction

Candace Parker's name is etched into the annals of basketball history as a force of nature, a woman whose career defied expectations and shattered them entirely. From her early days on the courts of St. Louis to her ascent as one of the brightest stars in the WNBA, Parker's journey has been marked by brilliance, resilience, and an unwavering commitment to excellence. But beyond the highlights and the accolades, Candace's story is one of profound transformation—a tale of breaking barriers, of overcoming the challenges that come with being a woman in a world still dominated by men, and of using her platform to advocate for change in ways that few athletes ever do.

When Candace Parker first picked up a basketball, it was clear that she was destined for greatness. Her natural talent was undeniable, and her rise to prominence was swift, culminating in an incredible college career at the University of Tennessee under the legendary Pat Summitt. But it wasn't just her skill that set her apart—her unshakable mental toughness, her ability to lead with poise and passion, and her drive to be more than just a player. Candace understood from the beginning that basketball was not just about winning; it was about changing the game, about pushing the boundaries of what was possible for women in sports.

Entering the WNBA in 2008, Candace was already a household name. But as she stepped onto the professional stage, it became clear that the challenges she would face went far beyond what could be measured in points or rebounds. The WNBA was still a league in its infancy, struggling to gain the recognition and respect that its male counterpart enjoyed. Yet, in many ways, Candace became the bridge between the league's early struggles and its growth into the cultural powerhouse it is today. She didn't just play the game; she transformed it. With every season, Candace brought a level of skill and leadership that inspired her teammates, earned her fans, and elevated the league to new heights. She became the face of the WNBA, a role that she took on with grace, responsibility, and an unrelenting desire to break down the barriers that continued to hold women in sports back.

Candace Parker's legacy is more than just a collection of championships, MVP awards, and All-Star selections. Her impact stretches far beyond the confines of the court, extending into the world of media, business, and social advocacy. She was a trailblazer—not just in her sport but in the world of women's rights, equality, and representation. She was an advocate for pay equity, for better media coverage of women's sports, and for a future where the accomplishments of female athletes were celebrated as fervently as those of their male counterparts. Through her platform, Candace demanded more—not just for herself, but for all women in sports. She refused to let her success be defined by the limitations placed on her by a society that had long undervalued the contributions of female athletes.

Yet, despite the public accolades and the recognition, Candace's journey was not without its struggles. The balance between a grueling professional career and her personal life—her family, relationships, and motherhood—was a constant challenge. Candace, like so many other athletes, had to grapple with the sacrifices that come with being at the top of her game. The demands of travel, training, and competition often left little room for the normalcy of life, and Candace was forced to navigate the emotional toll of being away from her loved ones, the pressure of constantly being in the public eye, and the struggle to maintain a sense of self amid the chaos. Her personal life, though often hidden from the spotlight, was as rich and complex as her professional career. She was more than just an athlete—she was a daughter, a sister, a mother, and a friend, each role carrying its own set of joys and heartaches.

In this book, we explore not only the triumphs that defined Candace Parker's legendary career but also the challenges that shaped her into the woman she is today. We delve into her transformation from a young basketball prodigy to a global icon, examining the obstacles she faced along the way and how she overcame them with grace and determination. This is a story not just of success, but of the personal journey of a woman who refused to be defined by anything other than her ambition, her own will, and her strength. It is a story of breaking barriers—of refusing to accept the limitations that society places on women and athletes, and of carving a new path for future generations.

Candace's impact on the WNBA is immeasurable. She was a key figure in bringing the league into the mainstream, a leader who elevated the game and inspired millions with her talent, resilience, and advocacy. But her influence goes beyond basketball. She is a role model for women everywhere, showing that greatness is not limited by gender and that the strength to overcome obstacles is within us all. Candace's journey is one of triumph and transformation, of breaking down barriers, and of reimagining what it means to be a woman in sports.

As Candace transitions from playing to other endeavors, her legacy will continue to influence the world of sports and beyond. She is no longer just a basketball player—she is a powerful voice for change, a leader in the fight for equality, and a shining example of what it means to push past limitations and strive for something greater than oneself. Candace Parker's story is far from over, but her impact on the world will resonate for generations to come.

This book is not just a chronicle of a basketball legend; it is a testament to the power of determination, the strength of character, and the courage to challenge the status quo. Candace Parker's journey is a powerful reminder that no dream is too big, no barrier too strong, and no challenge too great to overcome. Through every victory and every setback, Candace Parker has shown us what it means to rise, to lead, and to leave a lasting legacy. Her story is one of inspiration, of resilience, and of the relentless pursuit of excellence—on and off the court.

Chapter 1:
The Early Years
From St. Louis to Stardom

From the moment Candace Parker first gripped a basketball, the trajectory of her life began to carve its extraordinary path, one that would soon lead her to become a legend on and off the court. It's often said that greatness has a way of revealing itself in the most unlikely places, and for Candace, it began in the city of St. Louis, Missouri—a place where dreams were born, but only through grit and perseverance. Hers was a story that no one could have fully predicted, a tale of resilience, ambition, and destiny.

Candace's world was defined by the pace of competition. The Parker family, though not wealthy, was rich in the kind of intangible assets that are necessary to rise above mediocrity: determination, hard work, and an unshakeable belief in each other. Her father, Larry, had been an athlete, a gifted basketball player who never quite made it to the heights he had hoped for. But rather than seeing his athletic dreams go unrealized as a failure, Larry Parker channeled his unfulfilled ambitions into something more powerful: the nurturing of a legacy, a calling passed down through his daughter. A man of few words but fierce conviction, Larry saw in Candace a promise not just to play the game, but to change the very way it was played by women. He saw her potential, and from the earliest years, he placed her on a court where she could dream big.

Her mother, Sara, also had been an athlete—an accomplished tennis player. She was both an anchor of stability and a source of inspiration. While Larry instilled in Candace the drive to compete, it was Sara who taught her the value of discipline and balance, imparting wisdom that would eventually make Candace not only a world-class athlete but also a woman capable of handling the rigors of fame, the weight of responsibility, and the challenges of constant scrutiny. Sara had also been a teacher, and her understanding of structure and organization ensured Candace was never overwhelmed by the challenges that lay ahead. As much as Candace was drawn to the world of athletics, she was equally motivated by her mother's insistence on excelling in academics—another field where she would, inevitably, distinguish herself.

As a child, Candace was a study in contrasts. On one hand, she was quiet, a thinker who loved the stillness of books and the company of a world that often seemed too loud for her. On the other hand, once she set foot on the basketball court, that quiet exterior vanished. Candace became a force. She was a natural athlete, but it wasn't just physical prowess that made her stand out. It was the fierce desire to win, to outwork, to outsmart her opponents, a determination that would be evident throughout her entire career. She had a deep, almost innate understanding of the game. Basketball wasn't just about the physicality of the sport for Candace; it was a mental chess match that she could play better than anyone else.

From an early age, Candace didn't just play basketball—she dominated. In the schoolyard, among friends and peers, she stood out. No one questioned her ability, and soon, no one dared to challenge her. But it wasn't just her physical strength that turned heads; it was the quiet intensity with which she approached every game. Candace didn't speak much about her abilities; rather, she let her performance do the talking. By the time she was in middle school, coaches from local teams had begun to notice her. It wasn't long before her skills caught the attention of bigger leagues, and the dream of playing college basketball seemed less of a fantasy and more of a reality.

Though she was already excelling on the court, Candace still faced one of the most difficult barriers any young athlete encounters: the challenge of balancing athletic ambition with academic success. The Parker family understood that without a solid education, no athletic career would be sustainable. They were unwavering in their support for Candace's academic pursuits, insisting that she remain grounded in her studies even as she began to rise through the ranks of young basketball talent. Her natural intelligence shone both in the classroom and on the court, making it clear early on that Candace would not only be a star player, but also a multifaceted individual—one who could handle the pressures of being a top athlete while maintaining her integrity as a student.

Her high school years were marked by a relentless pursuit of perfection. Candace attended Naperville Central High School, where she quickly became a star on the court. She didn't just want to be good; she wanted to be the best. And so, she pushed herself beyond the limits of what many thought was possible. By the time she was a sophomore, Candace was already averaging double digits in points and rebounds. Her presence on the court was undeniable, and soon enough, the whispers of her talent grew louder, eventually reaching coaches from across the country. Every time Candace stepped onto the court, it was as though the world faded away, leaving only the game. There was no fear of failure, no hesitation, just the instinct to perform—to make a statement.

Despite her talent, Candace was never consumed by arrogance. She remained humble, aware of the responsibilities that came with her newfound fame. Her journey was still just beginning, and Candace knew that it would take more than just natural talent to rise to the top. It would require dedication, sacrifice, and a deep, unwavering belief in herself. Candace was driven not by the pursuit of fame, but by the desire to prove something—to herself, to her family, and the world that she could be a trailblazer in a sport that often overlooked women. She wasn't just aiming for success in basketball; she was setting the stage for a legacy.

Her time at Naperville Central was a testament to her growing potential. But it was also a time when the weight of the world began to feel more tangible. Candace faced pressure like few athletes do. Expectations mounted as she became a household name, but it didn't seem to faze her. What might break others, Candace used as fuel. She was learning the delicate balance between confidence and humility, between the ferocious desire to win and the wisdom to remain grounded. It was a balance that would serve her well in the years to come.

In a city like St. Louis, where dreams can fade as quickly as they appear, Candace Parker's path to greatness was anything but assured. But through the unwavering support of her family and her relentless drive, Candace was positioning herself for something much greater than anyone could have imagined. At the dawn of her high school career, Candace's name was already on the lips of coaches and analysts alike, but the real test was yet to come. Her talent, her intelligence, and her hunger for success would soon push her to the next chapter of her life, where the dream of playing at the highest level was no longer just a vision—it was a certainty.

In those early years, Candace Parker wasn't just a girl with dreams of playing basketball. She was already becoming a symbol of what it meant to push beyond limits, to shatter the ceilings that had been placed above her. In a world where opportunities for women in sports were often restricted, Candace was laying the foundation for a career that would not only break barriers but also redefine what it meant to be a woman in basketball. Her early years in St. Louis were marked by one thing above all else: the birth of a champion. A champion whose journey would soon captivate the world.

Chapter 2:
The College Years
Tennessee & Pat Summitt

Candace Parker's transition from the bustling streets of St. Louis to the grand, rolling hills of Knoxville, Tennessee, was a leap that not only defined her as an athlete but also set the stage for the profound impact she would have on the sport of basketball. In the heart of the South, at the University of Tennessee, Candace would find herself in the crucible of greatness, under the tutelage of one of the most iconic figures in women's basketball history: Pat Summitt. The story of her time in Tennessee is not merely about the accolades she amassed, but about the profound transformation she underwent as a player, as a woman, and as a symbol of what it means to break barriers.

The day Candace Parker arrived on the campus of the University of Tennessee, she was already a household name in the world of college basketball, a prodigy whose talents seemed limitless. But the world of collegiate athletics would prove to be a world of its own, full of both promise and pressure, where the road to greatness is never paved without challenge. Candace, though, had the heart of a warrior, and in the face of overwhelming expectation, she remained undaunted.

From the very start, Candace's arrival in Knoxville was met with both excitement and skepticism. The expectations placed on her were immense—she was expected to elevate Tennessee's already storied program to even greater heights. But for Candace, the weight of these expectations was not a burden to carry but a driving force. She arrived in Tennessee with one singular focus: to win and to prove that she belonged at the highest level. Yet, despite the public accolades and the media attention that followed her every move, Candace was determined to remain grounded, to focus not on the spotlight but on the game itself. For all her talent, Candace had the humility and poise to recognize that her journey was just beginning.

Her first encounter with Pat Summitt would shape the course of Candace's life. Summitt, a woman whose name was synonymous with excellence, was known for her no-nonsense approach and her ability to push players beyond what they thought possible. Summitt was not someone who relied on smooth words or easy praise—she demanded nothing short of perfection. The intensity with which Summitt coached was the stuff of legend, and it was immediately clear to Candace that this was a woman who wouldn't coddle her, who wouldn't allow her to rest on her laurels. Summitt's coaching style was rigorous and unyielding, but it was precisely what Candace needed.

At first, Candace struggled with the tough love that Pat Summitt dispensed in abundance. Coming from a family where support had always been strong but never overbearing, Candace had not yet encountered a coach who pushed her as hard as Summitt did. But what Candace didn't know then was that Pat Summitt was not simply looking to build a great player; she was looking to build a champion, someone who could shoulder the expectations not just for themselves, but for an entire program. Summitt saw in Candace not only immense talent but the raw material of greatness. But greatness required more than skill; it required mental toughness, discipline, and the willingness to fight through adversity. Summitt was ready to show Candace just how far those qualities could take her.

There were moments of tension, moments where Candace questioned her ability to meet Summitt's high standards. There were days when Candace felt the weight of the world on her shoulders, as the demands of college basketball, academics, and the pressures of being one of the most talked-about athletes in the country began to take their toll. But Candace, true to her nature, pushed forward. She listened, she learned, and slowly, she began to understand what it was that Pat Summitt had seen in her from the start. Summitt was shaping Candace into a player who could do more than just score points; she was shaping Candace into a player who could lead, who could inspire, who could carry a team to the highest levels of success.

As the months passed, Candace's transformation was evident. Her game evolved beyond the raw athleticism that had made her a star in high school. She became a more strategic player, learning to read the flow of the game, to anticipate her opponents' moves, and to make decisions in real-time that demonstrated a level of maturity far beyond her years. Under Summitt's watchful eye, Candace developed into a player who was not only capable of taking over a game but who could do so while also making her teammates better. She became the leader of the Tennessee Lady Vols, not by being the loudest voice in the room, but by being the one who could be relied upon to make the right play at the right time. Her leadership was silent but powerful—a quiet force that carried the team through difficult moments and lifted them to greatness.

Tennessee's success during Candace's years there was nothing short of extraordinary. Under Summitt's guidance, the Lady Vols dominated the NCAA landscape. Candace led the team to a national title in 2007, the culmination of years of hard work, sacrifice, and dedication. The win was not just a personal triumph for Candace; it was a validation of all the sacrifices she and her teammates had made, all the hours spent in the gym, all the bruises and bumps that had been part of the journey. For Candace, winning the national championship was a moment of reflection—a recognition that all the struggles, all the tough practices, all the moments of doubt had been worth it. The victory was not just a testament to her skill, but to her resilience, her perseverance, and her refusal to let anything stand in her way.

But even in such glory, Candace's journey at Tennessee was far from simple. College life, particularly for an athlete of her caliber, was fraught with its own unique set of challenges. The balance between athletics, academics, and the demands of being a public figure was a tightrope walk. Candace was constantly in the spotlight, and every move she made was scrutinized, every victory celebrated, every loss analyzed. Yet, through it all, she remained focused on her goals. She was driven not by the need for attention or accolades, but by the desire to be the best. And this desire, this unyielding commitment to excellence, is what set Candace apart from so many of her peers.

Her time at Tennessee was also marked by the relationships she built with her teammates, friendships that would last long after her college days were over. Candace was never a player who sought to elevate herself at the expense of others; she was a team player through and through. She understood that success in basketball was never an individual endeavor—it was about working together, supporting each other, and lifting the entire team to new heights. It was this mentality that made her not just a great player but a great leader. Her humility and generosity of spirit shone through in every practice, every game, and every moment of her college career.

Looking back on her time at Tennessee, Candace would come to realize that her college years were more than just a stepping stone to a professional career—they were the foundation upon which her entire legacy was built. It was in Tennessee that Candace truly began to understand what it meant to be a champion, to carry the weight of expectation, and to use it as fuel to drive her forward. It was in Tennessee that Candace became a household name, and it was in Tennessee that she first experienced the profound satisfaction that comes from achieving something greater than oneself.

Candace's years in Knoxville were marked by both triumph and struggle, joy and sacrifice, but they were also the years when she truly came into her own as a player and as a person. And as she looked toward the future, toward a professional career that was already calling her name, she knew that the lessons she had learned under Pat Summitt's watchful eye would serve her well in whatever came next.

Chapter 3:
Entering the WNBA
A New Era Begins

Candace Parker's entry into the WNBA was nothing short of historic. It was a moment that marked not only the beginning of her professional basketball career but also a new chapter in the evolution of the league itself. The year was 2008, and the WNBA had already established itself as a premier professional women's sports league, but there was a sense that something truly transformative was on the horizon. Candace Parker, the electrifying young star from the University of Tennessee, was about to make her long-anticipated debut. The hype surrounding her was palpable, not merely because of her immense talent, but because of the promise she held to reshape the game for women in a way that had never been seen before.

From the moment Candace was selected by the Los Angeles Sparks as the first overall pick in the 2008 WNBA Draft, the stage was set for her to redefine what it meant to be a professional female athlete. The world was watching. Expectations were not just high; they were astronomical. Candace had become a national figure in women's basketball, largely due to her dynamic performances at Tennessee, where she had earned accolades like the NCAA Player of the Year and led her team to an NCAA championship. But now, she was stepping into the world of professional basketball, where the stakes were infinitely higher, and the competition far fiercer. The pressure on her shoulders was almost suffocating, yet it was a pressure she had known how to carry since she was a young girl in St. Louis, trying to prove herself among her peers.

The Los Angeles Sparks, a franchise steeped in history and prestige, had made a clear statement with the selection of Parker. They were betting on her not only to be the centerpiece of their team but to serve as the spark that would elevate the entire league. The task ahead was monumental: to guide the Sparks to championships while bearing the weight of a league that was desperate for its next icon. But Candace, ever determined, was not one to shrink away from challenges; she welcomed them. There was no question in her mind that she was ready.

The transition from college to the professional ranks is one that few truly understand unless they have lived it. College basketball, for all its intensity, is a different beast entirely from the WNBA. The level of competition, the physicality, the expectations—everything was more intense, more demanding. And for Candace, this was not simply about adjusting to a new style of play or learning to coexist with a new set of teammates. This was about embracing a new identity. The world knew Candace Parker, but in the WNBA, she was just another player trying to prove herself all over again. The question was not whether she had the talent—everyone knew she did—but whether she had the fortitude to handle the pressure that comes with being the face of a league.

It didn't take long for Candace to prove herself. Her rookie season was nothing short of spectacular. From the very first game, she showed the WNBA—and the world—that she was not just a rising star; she was a force to be reckoned with. Her debut on June 6, 2008, against the Phoenix Mercury was one for the ages. Candace walked into that arena with a sense of calm, despite the frenzied atmosphere, and displayed a level of skill and poise that belied her inexperience. She scored 34 points and grabbed 12 rebounds, becoming the youngest player in league history to achieve such a feat. The basketball world was stunned. This was not just a promising rookie; this was a future superstar, and her impact was immediate.

But while the individual accolades piled up for Candace—her first WNBA All-Star selection, Rookie of the Year honors, and an MVP award—all of it seemed secondary to the larger goal that had been placed on her shoulders: to elevate the Sparks to championship glory. The stakes were high, and Candace's desire to win was insatiable. She had tasted victory at the collegiate level, but the world of professional sports was different. Championships in the WNBA were hard-earned, and nothing was given. But Candace's competitive spirit, forged in the fires of Pat Summitt's coaching and honed through years of playing against the best, was exactly what the Sparks needed. She was not just a player; she was a leader, a game-changer.

Her rookie season was a wild success for the Sparks, but it wasn't without its challenges. As expected, the pressure to perform at such a high level was a constant presence. The attention from the media, the fans, and even her teammates was unrelenting. Candace had to quickly learn how to navigate the pressure and focus on what mattered most: her game. She leaned heavily on the guidance of her coach, Michael Cooper, and her veteran teammates, such as Lisa Leslie, whose leadership and experience helped ease Candace's transition into the pro ranks. But despite the invaluable mentorship of her teammates, Candace knew that she was forging her path. The spotlight on her was blinding, but she used it to her advantage, channeling the attention into a fierce determination to succeed.

The months that followed were a whirlwind of growth, both personally and professionally. Candace continued to play with the poise and precision that had made her a star at Tennessee, but now, she was learning the nuances of professional basketball—the chess match of the game, the intricacies of strategy, and the importance of being able to perform under pressure. Her athleticism was undeniable, but Candace's growth as a player was defined not by what she could do physically, but by how she adapted to the mental side of the game. The mental toughness required to excel in the WNBA was far different from anything Candace had encountered in college. But she rose to the occasion, consistently playing at an elite level and proving that she was not just a talented player but a relentless competitor who could perform when it mattered most.

In her first season, Candace helped lead the Sparks to the Western Conference finals, a thrilling but ultimately heartbreaking series that ended with a loss to the San Antonio Silver Stars. It was a painful experience, but one that served as a defining moment in Candace's career. The loss stung deeply, but it also solidified her resolve. She was not satisfied with individual accolades. She wanted championships. She wanted to be remembered as someone who not only dominated the court but who led her team to greatness. That first season was a reminder that success in the WNBA didn't come easily, and the journey to a championship was a long and arduous one. But Candace was willing to do whatever it took to get there.

By the time Candace Parker's second season in the WNBA arrived, it was clear that her place in the league was solidified. She had become the face of the Sparks, the centerpiece of their championship aspirations. The stakes were higher now—expectations for her and the team had grown exponentially. And while the team fell short of a title in her second season, it was clear that Candace was not a player who could be defined by the outcome of a single season. Her resilience, her ability to overcome adversity, and her drive to continue evolving as a player became the hallmark of her career.

Candace Parker's entry into the WNBA was not just the start of a career; it was the dawn of a new era. She was more than just a player—she was a symbol of possibility, a beacon for young athletes who dreamed of breaking through the barriers that had long restricted women in sports. Her presence in the league brought new attention, new respect, and new energy to women's basketball. She had become a force not just on the court, but in the culture of the sport itself. Candace Parker was no longer just an athlete; she was an icon, and the world was just beginning to understand the magnitude of what she would achieve. Her journey was just beginning, and it was clear that her impact on the game would be felt for generations to come.

Chapter 4: Breaking Barriers Personal and Professional Struggles

Candace Parker's journey to greatness was never going to be an easy one. She had the talent, the work ethic, and the will to succeed, but there were challenges ahead that she couldn't have predicted—the weight of expectations, the limitations placed on women in sports, and the deep, often unspoken struggles that come with being a woman at the pinnacle of a male-dominated profession. It was in these moments of personal and professional turmoil that Candace would come to define herself, not just as a player, but as a symbol of resilience, strength, and the quiet power of breaking through barriers.

The early years of Candace's professional career were filled with triumph and adulation. From her breathtaking debut to her rapidly rising status as one of the WNBA's brightest stars, the world seemed to be at her feet. Yet beneath the surface, Candace was already beginning to feel the pull of an ever-increasing pressure—an invisible weight that came with being thrust into the spotlight at such a young age. There was an undeniable joy in her success, but there was also a profound sense of isolation. The very thing that made her stand out—her extraordinary talent—was the same thing that set her apart from others, making her feel distanced and alone in a world that was still reluctant to accept women at the top.

On the court, Candace was a revelation. She was a player unlike any the league had ever seen—her athleticism, her basketball IQ, her leadership, and her quiet confidence made her the face of a new era in women's basketball. But off the court, Candace was learning the difficult lesson that the world of sports, particularly women's sports, didn't always embrace the same sense of fairness and equity that it pretended to uphold. As a woman in a male-dominated industry, Candace was already encountering the many barriers that women athletes have always faced: the pay disparities, the scrutiny of her every move, and the constant need to prove herself—not just as a basketball player, but as a worthy adversary to the male athletes whose fame and fortune dwarfed her own. Candace was expected to lead, to perform, and to inspire, but she was never given the same privileges and allowances that her male counterparts received. There was no room for mistakes, no tolerance for weakness, and certainly no celebration of the very human nature of her struggles.

In this whirlwind, Candace found herself grappling with not just external pressure but the internal challenges that came with carrying the hopes and expectations of an entire generation on her shoulders. The weight of representation was heavy. Candace was not simply Candace Parker, a young woman trying to find her way in the world; she was *the* Candace Parker, the face of the WNBA, the athlete who could single-handedly change the narrative for women in sports. And with that role came the unspoken understanding that she had to be perfect. There was no room for vulnerability, no space for error. Every time she stepped onto the court, she wasn't just representing herself or her team—she was representing an entire movement.

The professional struggles were compounded by personal ones. Despite her success, Candace was often seen through a lens that was far from kind. For all of her talent, her confidence, and her unwavering focus, Candace faced the kind of criticism and judgment that is uniquely reserved for women in sports. Every aspect of her life was dissected by the public eye—her appearance, her demeanor, her relationships, and her decisions. She was subjected to scrutiny in a way that few male athletes would ever experience, and it took a toll on her. The pressure to constantly meet the world's expectations of perfection weighed heavily on her mental health and sense of self.

The stress of being scrutinized so intensely and the emotional toll of constantly being in the public eye led Candace to a point where she had to take a hard look at herself and her career. There were times when she questioned her worth, doubted her place in a world that seemed set up for her to fail, and wondered if all the sacrifices were worth it. It was in these moments of vulnerability that Candace found her true strength—not in deflecting the pressure or hiding from it, but in facing it head-on, acknowledging the weight of it, and deciding to move forward, no matter the cost. She had become accustomed to silencing her doubts for the sake of her career, but now, she began to listen to the quieter, more personal voices-the ones that spoke of balance, of peace, and of the need to nurture her well-being amidst the chaos.

It was during this period of personal introspection that Candace realized that her greatest struggles were not just external, but internal. The battle was not only against the expectations of the world, but against the relentless drive within her that demanded more and more. She had been so focused on achieving the next goal, on meeting the next challenge, that she had lost sight of what truly mattered to her.

She wasn't just fighting for herself or her team; she was fighting for the image of herself that she had projected to the world. And it was in the process of deconstructing that image, of allowing herself to be human, that Candace began to find a new sense of peace.

The journey to self-acceptance was neither quick nor easy. It involved a willingness to confront not only the external barriers that stood in her way but the internal barriers that had been built over years of striving, of pushing, and of denying herself the space to breathe. It was a long road, one that was fraught with moments of doubt, insecurity, and fear. But through it all, Candace remained resolute. She would not let the world define her. She would not let the narrow confines of expectation dictate who she was or what she could achieve. She would break through, not just the physical barriers that existed within the sport, but the emotional and psychological barriers that had held her captive for so long.

Her struggles were not only a part of her evolution, but they also became a source of strength for others. Candace's vulnerability, her willingness to confront her imperfections, became a beacon for women in sports, for athletes of all kinds who were struggling to balance their professional lives with their identities. Candace understood, perhaps better than anyone, that true greatness was not about being perfect—it was about persevering in the face of imperfection, about learning to love oneself even when the world demanded more. She became not just an icon of basketball but a symbol of strength, resilience, and the quiet power of owning one's story.

As she navigated the complexities of fame, success, and the weight of being a role model, Candace Parker found that the real victory lay not in championships or accolades, but in the ability to stand firm in her truth. The struggles she faced, both personal and professional, had shaped her into the woman she had always wanted to become—someone who could inspire, not by being flawless, but by showing others that the road to success is often paved with difficulty, and that true strength comes from the ability to rise after every fall.

Candace Parker's story is not just one of athletic achievement; it is a story of breaking barriers—of pushing through limitations, both external and internal. It is a story of confronting the darkness within and finding the light. And it is a story of resilience, of standing tall even when the world seems to be trying to push you down. The barriers Candace broke were not just physical ones; they were the emotional, psychological, and societal barriers that have long held women in sports back. And in breaking those barriers, Candace Parker not only transformed the game of basketball but also redefined what it means to be a woman in a world that often asks for more than one can give.

Chapter 5: The Champion's Mindset Mental Toughness and Resilience

Candace Parker's rise to the pinnacle of professional basketball was not a mere product of natural talent or physical prowess; it was the result of a mental fortitude so unwavering, so resolute, that it would come to define not only her career but the very essence of what it means to be a champion. In a sport where the margins between victory and defeat are razor-thin, Candace learned early on that mental toughness was the bedrock of success. It was not enough to simply possess the skills or the athleticism; it was the ability to dig deep in moments of adversity, to withstand pressure when everything seemed to be crumbling around her, that would ultimately determine her legacy.

Mental toughness is often misunderstood. It is not simply the ability to power through pain or persevere when the body is fatigued. It is about mastery of the mind, the ability to control your thoughts, emotions, and focus in the face of overwhelming odds. Candace Parker learned this lesson in a way few athletes ever do—by overcoming setbacks that might have broken lesser players, by embracing the difficult moments and using them to fuel her drive rather than to define her. Her journey was not a linear ascent to the top, but a winding path marked by moments of doubt, failure, and resilience that only served to deepen her resolve.

Her rookie season in the WNBA was a testament to her innate resilience. Coming off a stellar college career at Tennessee, Candace had already garnered the kind of attention that few young athletes ever experience. But as she stepped into the professional arena, the expectations grew exponentially. The weight of the WNBA's future rested squarely on her shoulders. There was a sense that she was not just playing for herself, but for an entire generation of women in sports. Every mistake, every miss, every stumble would be magnified, and Candace was acutely aware of the stakes. Yet, rather than shrinking from the pressure, she embraced it. Her debut was nothing short of remarkable—34 points and 12 rebounds, a performance that announced her arrival with the kind of bang that the basketball world could not ignore. But this triumph was only the beginning. The real test would come in the weeks and months that followed, when the grind of a professional career, coupled with the pressure of constant expectation, began to take its toll.

It is easy to see success in athletes like Candace and believe that they are somehow immune to doubt or fear, but the truth is far more human. Candace had her moments of insecurity, of questioning whether she truly belonged among the stars. There were games when she missed shots, made turnovers, or simply couldn't find her rhythm. These were the moments that tested her mental resolve—the moments that, if left unchecked, could have unraveled her. But Candace had something that separated her from so many others: the ability to block out the noise, to focus on what was within her control, and to keep moving forward. She didn't allow the inevitable failures of the game to dictate her worth; she used them as opportunities for growth, seeing each setback as a lesson rather than a defeat.

As the years passed, Candace's understanding of mental toughness evolved. She began to realize that true champions are not defined by their victories alone, but by how they handle the moments that do not go according to plan. Championships, she learned, are not won in the easy moments, but in the hard ones—in the fourth quarter, with the game on the line, when everything seems to be falling apart and only the strongest minds can prevail. For Candace, the defining moments of her career were not always the highlight-reel plays or the accolades, but the quiet determination to rise above adversity and keep pushing, even when the odds seemed insurmountable.

One of the most pivotal lessons Candace learned came in the wake of her injuries. Throughout her career, Candace faced several physical setbacks—knee injuries, ankle sprains, and various strains that threatened to derail her progress. For any athlete, injuries are not just physical challenges; they are mental hurdles. They test one's resolve, the will to push through pain, the determination to return to the court stronger than before. In the face of these obstacles, Candace's resilience became even more apparent. Rather than allowing herself to wallow in frustration, she chose to embrace the rehabilitation process with the same tenacity that she brought to the game. She approached recovery as if it were a game in itself, setting goals, tracking progress, and relentlessly pursuing her return to form. The mental discipline required to overcome these setbacks was a testament to her unwavering commitment to her craft. She didn't see herself as a victim of her circumstances; instead, she saw each injury as an opportunity to grow stronger, not just physically, but mentally.

But Candace's resilience was not just about overcoming physical injury. It was about mental renewal, the ability to reset after a tough loss, to shake off the sting of failure, and to approach each new game with the same intensity and focus as the last. It was this mental reset, this refusal to dwell on past mistakes, that set Candace apart from her peers. She had learned the importance of letting go of the things she couldn't control—the missed shots, the turnovers, the bad calls—and instead focused on what she could control: her effort, her attitude, and her ability to inspire those around her.

Perhaps one of the most defining moments in Candace's career came during the 2016 WNBA season, when, after years of heartbreak, she led the Los Angeles Sparks to the championship. The path to that title was not a smooth one. The team had faced setbacks, injuries, and doubts throughout the season, but Candace's leadership and mental toughness proved to be the glue that held everything together. She had been in the league long enough to know that the road to a championship was not just about skill—it was about heart, about perseverance, and mental toughness. And when the final buzzer sounded in Game 5 of the Finals, with Candace's clutch play helping the Sparks secure their first title in 14 years, it was not just a victory for her; it was a victory for everything she had fought for—the countless hours of work, the sacrifices, the moments of doubt, and the unrelenting drive to prove that she was a champion, both on and off the court.

Candace's mental toughness was not just an innate gift—it was something she had cultivated over years of hard work, self-reflection, and a commitment to growth. It was forged in the fires of adversity, both personal and professional. Each time she faced a challenge, each time she overcame a setback, she grew stronger, more determined, more resilient. And as her career unfolded, it became clear that her mental toughness was just as crucial to her success as her physical abilities. Candace had learned, perhaps better than anyone, that greatness is not just about talent—it is about the ability to weather the storms, to rise when others would falter, and to keep moving forward when the world tells you to stop.

The champion's mindset that Candace Parker embodied was not something that came easily. It was the product of years of struggle, sacrifice, and an unwavering belief in herself and her ability to overcome whatever came her way. Her mental toughness was not just about holding it together when things were easy, but about thriving in the face of adversity, about turning obstacles into opportunities, and about pushing forward when everything seemed stacked against her. Candace Parker was, and remains, a testament to the power of resilience—the kind of resilience that is born not from the avoidance of hardship, but from the willingness to face it head-on, to keep fighting, and to emerge stronger on the other side.

Her journey wasn't just about basketball—it was about life. It was about showing up every day, giving everything you have, and refusing to let anything or anyone stand in your way. And in the end, it was this unwavering mindset, this relentless pursuit of excellence in the face of adversity, that would define Candace Parker as one of the greatest athletes and one of the most mentally tough competitors the world had ever seen.

Chapter 6:
The Glory Years
Rising to Prominence

Candace Parker's career was not just a story of athletic brilliance but a narrative of profound transformation, both on the court and within the broader context of women's sports. After stepping into the WNBA as its brightest new star, the journey that awaited her was one marked by challenges, triumphs, and a deepening legacy that would continue to reverberate through the sport for years to come. The early years were defined by growing pains and individual achievements, but it was during the glory years that Candace truly began to emerge as one of the greatest to ever play the game. It was during these years that she would redefine the expectations of what a player could achieve—both individually and as part of a team—and raise the profile of women's basketball to unprecedented heights.

The transition from prodigious talent to a true leader is never easy. But Candace's ascent was not about simple athleticism—it was about finding her identity as a player and understanding the weight of the responsibility that came with being the face of a franchise. For Candace, the stakes were never just about winning; they were about what winning could mean, not just for her, but for the entire league. As the star of the Los Angeles Sparks, Candace was thrust into a role that demanded leadership, resilience, and an unwavering commitment to excellence. The time had come for her to show the world what she was capable of—and more importantly, what the WNBA could become with a star of her caliber leading the charge.

It didn't take long for Candace to make her mark on the league. Her athleticism was unmatched, and her basketball IQ, honed under the watchful eye of Pat Summitt, was evident from the start. Yet, it wasn't just her ability to score, to rebound, or to dominate on the court that set her apart. Candace brought an intangible quality to the game—an aura of poise, focus, and composure that made her a natural leader. She was a player who could rise to the occasion, who could lead her team in the clutch moments when the game was on the line. And it was during these moments that Candace truly began to build her reputation as one of the most dominant forces in the history of the WNBA.

Candace's early years in the league were defined by a quest for something more than individual accolades. Though she quickly racked up honors and awards—becoming a multi-time All-Star, earning MVP honors, and leading her team to multiple playoff appearances—what she truly sought was a championship. Candace had experienced success at every level, from high school to college, but the pinnacle of her professional career had thus far eluded her. The heartbreak of falling short in the 2008 WNBA Finals to the Detroit Shock had ignited a fire within her that would fuel her relentless pursuit of that elusive title. It was a reminder that greatness was not measured in individual statistics or awards—it was measured in the ability to lead a team to the highest honor the game had to offer.

The journey to the 2016 championship was not a straight line. The path was filled with obstacles, both on and off the court. The Sparks had a roster full of talent, but success in the WNBA was never guaranteed. Injuries, roster changes, and the ever-present pressure of expectation created an atmosphere of uncertainty. But Candace, now a seasoned veteran, knew better than anyone that success was never about the absence of adversity—it was about how you responded to it. And in 2016, when the Sparks found themselves facing an uphill battle in the playoffs, it was Candace who rose to the occasion, leading her team with a fierce determination that had been honed over years of heartache and disappointment.

The 2016 WNBA Finals were the culmination of years of hard work, sacrifice, and growth. The series against the Minnesota Lynx, one of the most dominant teams in the history of the league, was a test of willpower, strength, and sheer resilience. Candace's performance in the Finals was nothing short of legendary. She played with a level of intensity and focus that lifted her teammates and ignited a spark within the entire organization. Every play, every shot, every rebound was infused with the energy of a player who knew what was at stake—and who was determined to see her team through to the other side.

In Game 5, with the series on the line, Candace delivered one of the most iconic performances of her career. She scored 28 points and grabbed 12 rebounds, leading the Sparks to a 77-76 victory and securing the team's first championship in 14 years. The moment was a culmination of everything Candace had worked for—a victory not just for her, but for the entire franchise, the city of Los Angeles, and the league itself. As the final buzzer sounded, Candace stood on the court, tears in her eyes, knowing that she had finally achieved the one thing that had eluded her throughout her career. She had done it—she had led her team to the top, and in doing so, she had cemented her place in the annals of basketball history.

But the glory years for Candace Parker were not defined solely by championships or accolades. They were also defined by her evolution as a player and as a leader. In the years following the 2016 championship, Candace's game continued to evolve. She was no longer simply the young phenom who had taken the league by storm in 2008. She had become a seasoned veteran, a leader on and off the court, whose influence extended far beyond the game itself. Candace had found her voice—not just as a player, but as an advocate for change, for equality, and for the advancement of women's sports. She was no longer just a basketball player; she was a role model, a mentor, and a trailblazer who was using her platform to make a difference.

Candace's impact extended far beyond her play on the court. She became one of the most visible and vocal advocates for women's basketball, using her position as a star athlete to push for greater recognition, better pay, and more opportunities for women in sports. As the face of the WNBA, Candace's influence was immeasurable. She pushed for systemic change, advocating for women to receive the same respect, recognition, and financial compensation that their male counterparts received in other sports. Her voice became an important part of the conversation surrounding the future of women's sports, and her advocacy helped pave the way for the next generation of athletes to step into a world where their value was recognized and respected.

The glory years were not just about basketball—they were about Candace's broader impact on the world of sports and culture. She became an ambassador for the game, a representative of the strength, resilience, and beauty that women athletes bring to the world. As her career continued to unfold, Candace became a symbol of the potential for women's sports to evolve into something far more significant, far more recognized, and far more respected than it had ever been before. She was no longer just a part of the league; she was its heart and soul.

By the time Candace Parker reached the height of her career, she had become more than just a basketball player—she had become a force of nature, a cultural icon who transcended the game itself. The glory years were not just marked by on-court accomplishments but by the profound impact she had on the sport of basketball and the world beyond. Her influence stretched across generations, inspiring young athletes to dream bigger, to fight harder, and to believe that anything was possible. Candace Parker had become more than a champion—she had become a symbol of what it meant to rise to the occasion, to face adversity head-on, and to leave a legacy that would resonate for years to come.

The story of Candace Parker is one of unparalleled success, relentless pursuit, and an unwavering belief in her ability to overcome any obstacle. It is a story of how greatness is not defined by the moments of triumph, but by the challenges faced along the way, and how, through resilience and determination, a true champion rises. And for Candace, the glory years were just the beginning—her journey was one of constant evolution, of breaking new ground, and of redefining the role of women in sports. The world would never forget the name Candace Parker, and the impact she made on the game would be felt for generations to come.

Chapter 7:
The Sky's the Limit
A New Chapter in Chicago

In the world of professional sports, transitions are often seen as pivotal moments, the turning of a page in a storied career. For Candace Parker, the decision to leave the city of Los Angeles, where she had built her legacy with the Sparks, and join the Chicago Sky was nothing short of a bold new beginning. It wasn't just a change of scenery—it was the start of a new chapter, a fresh challenge, and a chance to rewrite her story in a different city with a different team. For many athletes, such a move could feel like an unwelcome shift in momentum, but for Candace, it was an opportunity to evolve, to prove that her greatness was not bound by geography or history, but by her relentless drive and unwavering ambition. In Chicago, she found not only a new home but a place where her leadership, skill, and experience could help bring a long-awaited championship to a franchise that had been knocking on the door for years.

When Candace Parker signed with the Chicago Sky in 2021, the basketball world took notice. The signing was more than just a headline; it was a statement. It was a signal that Candace, at the height of her career, was still hungry for greatness. Having already achieved so much with the Los Angeles Sparks, including a WNBA championship in 2016, MVP awards, and countless accolades, Candace could have easily chosen to ride into the twilight of her career in comfort, solidifying her place as one of the greatest players in the league's history. But that was never Candace's style. For her, comfort was the enemy of growth. She sought challenges, new opportunities to lead, and places where her presence could make an immediate impact. Chicago, with its dedicated fan base, a promising core of players, and a franchise hungry for success, was the perfect fit.

The transition was not without its difficulties, however. After spending so many years with the Sparks, Candace had forged deep bonds with her teammates, coaches, and the Los Angeles community. To leave that behind was a monumental decision, one that came with its own set of emotional challenges. The ties she had built over the years in Los Angeles were not easily severed. But Candace, always one to embrace change, quickly made herself at home in Chicago, immersing herself in the culture of a new team with a new set of goals. She joined a squad that had steadily improved over the years but had yet to break through to the pinnacle of the WNBA. The Chicago Sky, led by a new coach, James Wade, had developed into a team full of talented players, but they needed something more—something that only Candace Parker, with her championship pedigree and leadership experience, could provide.

As the 2021 season unfolded, it became clear that Candace was exactly what the Sky needed. Her presence on the court was immediate and undeniable. She brought a level of leadership that was both vocal and quiet, an understanding of the game that came from years of experience at the highest level, and a commitment to winning that was contagious. She didn't just score points or grab rebounds—Candace became the cornerstone of the Sky's championship aspirations, setting an example both in practice and during games of what it meant to be relentless, disciplined, and focused. She was no longer just a player; she was a mentor, a guide, and a stabilizing force in the locker room.

The partnership between Candace and her new teammates blossomed quickly. Players like Courtney Vandersloot, Allie Quigley, and Kahleah Copper flourished under her leadership. Candace's ability to elevate the performance of those around her was evident from the outset. She understood that the true measure of greatness was not just in her accomplishments but in how she could help her teammates reach new heights. Candace's role was not to dominate the ball or control every possession, but to create an environment where every player felt empowered to contribute to the team's success. Her selflessness on the court and her ability to make others better were traits that set her apart as a leader.

The chemistry between Candace and the Sky was palpable, but it wasn't just about the X's and O's. The team had a renewed sense of purpose, and Candace's arrival injected an infectious energy into the entire organization. She quickly established herself as a trusted voice in the locker room, offering advice, encouragement, and unwavering support to the younger players. Her approach was both tough and nurturing, a combination that resonated deeply with a team that had long been searching for the right formula to win it all. Candace was more than just a player—she was the anchor, the steady hand that kept the ship on course, even when the seas grew rough.

The 2021 WNBA season was a roller coaster for the Sky, full of highs and lows, but with Candace Parker leading the charge, they began to build momentum at the right time. The playoffs arrived, and Chicago found itself on a path to the Finals. The journey was not easy, as they faced stiff competition from the league's best, but the Sky had something that no other team could match—Candace's championship experience and unyielding will to win. The veteran presence she brought to the court was invaluable, particularly in the tough moments when the pressure mounted. In Game 4 of the Finals, Candace delivered a masterful performance that proved to be the turning point in the series. With the Sky leading the series 2-1, Candace helped seal the victory with a clutch shot and a key defensive stop, pushing the team to its first-ever WNBA championship.

The championship win was a crowning achievement not just for Candace Parker but for the entire Sky organization. For Candace, it was a moment of vindication, a reminder that her decision to come to Chicago had been the right one, and that her hunger for more—more growth, more challenges, more success—had paid off. The celebration that followed was as much for her journey as it was for the collective effort of the team. The joy in the locker room, the smiles of her teammates, and the pride of a city that had long supported its team were a reflection of the hard work and sacrifices that had gone into this moment. Candace had found her new home, and she had led the Sky to glory in a way that few could have imagined when she first arrived.

Yet, Candace's time in Chicago was more than just a one-off victory. It was a reaffirmation of her place among the greats of the game. The championship was the culmination of everything she had worked for over the years—a recognition of her perseverance, her leadership, and her ability to excel in the face of new challenges. But for Candace, it was also a moment to reflect on how far she had come. The road from St. Louis to Los Angeles, and now to Chicago, had been long and full of obstacles, but Candace had never wavered. She had always believed in herself, in her ability to adapt, to grow, and to conquer whatever came her way. The Sky's championship win was a testament to her resilience and her unwavering commitment to her craft.

In the years that followed, Candace's influence on the Chicago Sky would continue to resonate. The team had now set a new standard for excellence, and her role in shaping that legacy would not be forgotten. For Candace, Chicago had become more than just a new team—it had become a place where she could continue to evolve, to inspire, and to lead by example. Her impact on the city, the franchise, and the sport was immeasurable. Candace Parker's journey was not defined by one team or one city, but by the unwavering pursuit of greatness and the ability to lift others along the way.

The story of Candace Parker in Chicago was one of redemption, of new beginnings, and of the power of resilience. It was a reminder that no matter the stage of your career, no matter the challenges you face, there is always a new chapter waiting to be written. And for Candace, that chapter was filled with triumph, leadership, and the realization that no matter where she went, the sky was, indeed, the limit.

Chapter 8:
A Champion's Journey Challenges Beyond the Court

Candace Parker's journey was never confined to the boundaries of the basketball court. Her story, woven through the fabric of her life, was one of constant challenges, both on and off the hardwood. For a player as gifted as Candace, the spotlight was always on her. But what many did not see was the quiet struggle that accompanied the fame, the pressure, and the unrelenting expectations placed on her shoulders. To be a champion is to overcome the challenges beyond the game, to rise through obstacles that are often unseen by the public eye. And Candace, in her unwavering pursuit of excellence, had to face not only the rigors of her sport but also the difficult realities of navigating life as one of the most visible and influential women in the world of sports.

For Candace, basketball was always a means to an end. It was her passion, her way to escape, to express herself, and to connect with others. But over the years, it became clear that her platform extended far beyond what she could accomplish in a game. Candace's rise to prominence coincided with a broader shift in the visibility of women's sports, but with that visibility came a host of unique challenges. Candace found herself not only battling against the fiercest athletes in the world but also advocating for something much bigger than herself: equality, representation, and respect for women athletes. To be a champion meant more than just winning games—it meant using her platform to spark change, to push for a future where the accomplishments of women in sports were celebrated as much as those of their male counterparts.

As one of the most recognizable faces in the WNBA, Candace's life was rarely her own. Every moment, every action, was scrutinized by a public that expected her to be perfect, not just as a basketball player, but as a role model. It was a pressure that was impossible to escape, and for Candace, it became clear early on that she would never be allowed to simply be an athlete. She was expected to be everything at once—an icon, a symbol of strength, and a representative of an entire generation of women fighting for recognition in sports. The weight of this responsibility was often overwhelming. She was not just carrying the hopes of her team, but the hopes of young girls and women everywhere who dreamed of seeing someone like themselves succeed at the highest level.

But Candace was never one to shy away from responsibility. She embraced the mantle of leadership, even as it meant constantly navigating the complexities of balancing her public persona with her private life. The challenge was not just about basketball—it was about living up to the expectations of an entire culture. The constant balancing act between the fierce athlete on the court and the woman behind the scenes, trying to maintain her privacy, her relationships, and her sense of self, was a battle that Candace had to face every day.

It was not just the external pressure that was hard to bear. There were internal battles, too. The journey to the top was never without its sacrifices, and as Candace's career progressed, she began to feel the toll it was taking on her personal life. Relationships were strained, her time with family was limited, and the emotional toll of constant travel, competition, and media attention was unrelenting. The spotlight, once a symbol of triumph, often felt like a suffocating weight, one that left little room for the normal joys and challenges of everyday life. There were moments when Candace questioned her worth, when she wondered whether the sacrifices she was making were worth the accolades and the fame. But true to her resilient nature, she kept moving forward. She had never been one to shy away from difficulty, and the challenges she faced beyond the court only added to her determination to succeed.

One of the most profound challenges Candace faced was the constant struggle for equity in women's sports. The disparity between the opportunities available to male and female athletes had always been glaring, but as Candace's star rose, she became more determined to fight for change. The lack of media coverage, the lower salaries, the limited sponsorship opportunities—these were all obstacles that women in sports faced daily, and Candace was at the forefront of pushing for change. She used her platform to speak out about the inequalities within the WNBA, to challenge the way women athletes were treated, and to demand the recognition and respect that they deserved. It was a battle that often felt like an uphill climb, but Candace's resolve was unwavering. She knew that her success wasn't just about her legacy—it was about changing the narrative for all women in sports.

But even as she fought for change in the world of sports, Candace had to confront the challenges that came with being an athlete in the public eye. The constant media attention, the scrutiny of her every move, the rumors and gossip that seemed to swirl around her—these were the burdens of fame that

Candace had to learn to live with. It wasn't easy. There were times when the weight of the world felt too much to bear, when she wished for the privacy and normalcy that so many people took for granted. But Candace, ever the professional, learned to navigate the complexities of her public life with grace and resilience. She became adept at managing the attention, using it not only to further her career but to elevate the game of women's basketball and to advocate for issues that mattered to her.

In addition to her role as an athlete and advocate, Candace also became a mother, a role that added yet another layer of complexity to her already demanding life. The challenges of balancing motherhood with the demands of a professional sports career were ones that many athletes, particularly women, understood all too well. For Candace, it was an experience that brought with it both immense joy and profound difficulty. Being away from her child for long stretches, navigating the pressures of motherhood while also competing at the highest level, was a challenge that few could fully comprehend. Yet, Candace handled it with the same grace and resilience that had defined her career. She became not only a role model for young athletes but also for working mothers everywhere, showing them that it was possible to achieve greatness while maintaining a sense of family and connection.

Candace's journey was also marked by personal loss and grief. Throughout her career, she had to cope with the loss of loved ones, the deaths of close family members, and the emotional toll of such experiences. Yet, through it all, Candace maintained her focus, her drive, and her commitment to her craft. She understood that life, much like basketball, was full of unexpected challenges—some that could knock you down, and others that could define you. Candace faced each challenge head-on, learning not only to cope with the pain but to turn it into something that fueled her determination to succeed. Her ability to find strength in the face of adversity became one of the defining qualities of her character.

Her journey, as remarkable as it was on the court, was just as profound off it. Candace's ability to break down barriers in sports, her tireless advocacy for women's rights, and her resilience in the face of immense pressure and personal loss were testaments to the champion that she had become. She was not just a great basketball player—she was a symbol of what it meant to overcome, to rise, and to continue pushing forward despite the odds.

Candace Parker's life was not defined by the trophies, the accolades, or the moments of glory on the court. It was defined by the quiet strength, the resilience, and the unwavering commitment to her craft, her family, and her community. The challenges she faced beyond the court were the ones that truly shaped her into the woman she became—one who was not just a champion in the eyes of the world, but a champion in her own right, someone who inspired millions through her ability to persevere, to fight for change, and to live with purpose. Her journey was never just about basketball—it was about life, and the power of overcoming whatever challenges came her way.

Chapter 9:
The Final Stretch Navigating Retirement

As the sun sets on a career defined by brilliance, triumph, and unparalleled determination, there comes a time when even the greatest athletes must face the inevitable truth that their playing days are behind them. For Candace Parker, that moment came after years of dominating the basketball court, leading teams to championships, earning MVP awards, and redefining what it meant to be a woman in a male-dominated sport. Her transition from player to retiree was not just about stepping away from the game; it was about navigating a new chapter, one filled with uncertainty, reflection, and the immense task of redefining herself in a world where her identity had been built on basketball.

The final stretch is not just the end of a physical journey; it is the start of a mental and emotional journey that no athlete is ever fully prepared for. When Candace decided to retire, it wasn't the fanfare of her last game or the adulation of a crowd that weighed most heavily on her mind. It was the quiet realization that the sport that had been her life for so long— her passion, her escape, her purpose—would no longer define her every day. For Candace, it was never just about basketball. It was the ability to compete, to challenge herself, to be part of something larger than herself. But in this final stretch, she would have to learn how to live without that daily purpose.

For most of her life, basketball had been her anchor. From the moment she first dribbled a ball as a child in St. Louis to her meteoric rise through the ranks of high school, college, and the WNBA, Candace had always known who she was—an athlete. Her identity had been firmly tied to the game, to the courts where she could express her greatness and silence any doubts through her performances. The fans, the accolades, the trophies—these were all affirmations of the work she had poured into her craft. But with retirement knocking on the door, Candace had to wrestle with a new identity. Who was she without the game? What would life look like when the rhythm of practice, games, and the unrelenting pursuit of excellence was no longer her daily routine?

The decision to step away from the game was not made lightly. It was a process—one that Candace knew would be a mix of relief and sorrow. On one hand, she had given everything to basketball. She had played through injuries, heartbreak, and intense pressure. She had sacrificed time with her family, with her friends, and even with herself to achieve greatness. The idea of not having to fight through the daily grind, of not waking up each day with the weight of expectations, was undeniably appealing. But on the other hand, there was the loss of purpose, of the spotlight, and of a sense of belonging to something that had defined her for over a decade.

Candace spent months in contemplation, considering her future with the same meticulous attention to detail she had given to her basketball career. She wasn't just retiring from a sport—she was stepping into the unknown. It wasn't just about leaving behind the game itself; it was about leaving behind a life that had shaped her very existence. For years, Candace had been lauded for her talents, her leadership, and her mental fortitude on the court, but now she was faced with a different kind of challenge: learning how to live outside the world of basketball.

The first steps into retirement were often marked by an unexpected stillness. The frenetic pace of competition, the adrenaline of game days, the camaraderie of teammates—suddenly, all of that faded into the background. There were no more post-game interviews, no more locker room banter, no more drills or practices that pushed her to her physical limits. At first, Candace found herself at a loss. The clarity she once found in the game was replaced by an overwhelming sense of emptiness. There were no opponents to face, no trophies to chase. Instead, there was just the quiet realization that the athlete she had always known herself to be was now someone else.

But Candace's resilience, forged over years of overcoming obstacles, guided her through this transition. Just as she had learned to reinvent her game, to grow from failure and setbacks, she began to reinvent herself in this new chapter. The loss of one identity gave way to the possibility of discovering new facets of herself. She turned her attention to the next phase of her life, one that didn't require her to dribble or shoot a basketball to feel fulfilled. The world outside the court was full of possibilities, full of opportunities to apply the same drive, determination, and leadership that had made her a legend in the sport.

Candace's transition into retirement was also marked by an increased involvement in the community and media. Though she no longer played the game, her voice remained one of the most powerful in sports. She became an advocate for change, using her platform to continue pushing for gender equality in sports and to advocate for the next generation of women athletes. Candace had always been more than just a player—she was a leader, a mentor, and a voice for the voiceless. Even in retirement, she found ways to use her influence to shape the future of women's basketball, ensuring that the sacrifices made by those who came before her would not be forgotten.

The next step in Candace's journey came through the opportunities that arose in broadcasting and business. Her knowledge of the game, her ability to articulate complex basketball concepts, and her natural charisma made her a sought-after voice in sports media. Candace became a prominent analyst, offering expert commentary on games, providing insight into the intricacies of the sport, and continuing to be an influential figure in the basketball community. She took on roles that allowed her to stay connected to the sport she loved while also embracing the opportunity to explore new passions and avenues for personal growth.

But even as Candace flourished in her new roles, there were still moments when the finality of retirement hit her. The absence of the game, the absence of the teammates and coaches who had been her family for so many years, left a void that was hard to fill. Yet, Candace learned to find joy in the simplicity of life without the constant pressure of performance. She learned to appreciate the moments spent with her family, the time she could dedicate to her interests, and the ability to live life on her terms, free from the public gaze that had followed her throughout her career.

Candace's retirement was a journey of rediscovery. It was a process of letting go of what was familiar and embracing the unknown with the same courage that had defined her playing days. She learned that retirement did not mean the end of her influence or her relevance; it simply marked the beginning of a new chapter, one where her impact would be felt in different ways, from the media to philanthropy to mentoring young athletes. Her legacy, built on her achievements as an athlete, would continue to inspire, to push the boundaries of what women in sports could achieve, and to demonstrate that greatness does not end when the game does.

In the years that followed her retirement, Candace remained a symbol of resilience, leadership, and the power of reinvention. Her journey through retirement was not without its struggles, but it was a journey that allowed her to reflect on everything she had accomplished and everything that still lay ahead. Candace Parker had proven time and time again that she was more than just a basketball player. She was a force of nature, a champion who would continue to leave her mark on the world, whether on the court or beyond it. And as she looked back on her illustrious career, she knew that while one chapter had ended, the story of Candace Parker was far from over.

Chapter 10:
Impact on the WNBA Elevating Women's Sports

Candace Parker's influence on the WNBA is not merely a reflection of her exceptional skills on the basketball court but rather an intricate, enduring legacy of transformative leadership and relentless advocacy. She was, and continues to be, a beacon for not only her teammates but for the next generation of female athletes. To comprehend the full weight of her impact, it is essential to understand how Candace Parker's journey transcended the confines of the basketball court, embedding itself in the larger narrative of women's sports and, in turn, reshaping the very structure and future of the WNBA itself.

From the moment she entered the WNBA as the first overall pick in the 2008 Draft, there was an aura about Candace. A child prodigy, a generational talent, and, most significantly, a harbinger of change. Candace's remarkable achievements on the court were undeniable, but she could redefine the conversation surrounding women in sports that marked her as a true pioneer. Her impact was not simply about elevating the level of competition or increasing the visibility of the WNBA. Her influence extended far beyond those initial goals. She became the figurehead of a movement—a movement that was as much about advocating for women's visibility and respect in sports as it was about her prowess as an athlete.

The WNBA, from its inception, struggled to find the same kind of cultural resonance that its male counterpart, the NBA, had achieved. Despite its incredible talent and the dedication of its athletes, the WNBA was often relegated to the margins of the sports conversation. While the men's game exploded with media attention, sponsorship deals, and international recognition, the women's game continued to be overlooked. Candace was aware of this disparity. It was something that gnawed at her, something that challenged her deeply—how could the WNBA, with so many incredibly talented athletes, fail to garner the attention and respect it so clearly deserved? And as Candace's career progressed, so did her understanding that her success would not be defined solely by what she accomplished on the court. It was time for the league to shift, and Candace Parker would be a central force in that revolution.

Candace became not just an athlete in the WNBA; she became a symbol of what could be. Her rise to prominence coincided with a shift in the public's perception of female athletes—one that was rooted in breaking barriers and demanding respect. What Candace did so effortlessly was embody the essence of an athlete who did not simply exist in the sport for her glory. Instead, she took on the weight of an entire generation of women athletes whose collective voices had been silenced for too long. Candace was not merely playing the game; she was raising it to new heights, making it impossible to ignore the strength, dedication, and skill that women could bring to professional sports.

Her drive to change the culture surrounding women's basketball in the United States was not driven by ego, but by the recognition that women in sports deserved equal recognition, equal resources, and the same platforms as men. Candace was aware of her position, and she wielded it with purpose. She began advocating for fair pay, better media coverage, and more sponsorships for WNBA players. The fight for pay equity in women's sports was one Candace took on with the same tenacity she brought to every game, every practice. She knew that the next generation of female athletes would look to the WNBA, to the players, and the league's structure for guidance. And she was determined that what she had to offer would not just be a legacy of championships and accolades, but one of systemic change—a promise that the barriers that existed would no longer stand unchallenged.

Candace was a vocal advocate for the league's growth, regularly calling attention to the disparities that kept the WNBA from flourishing to its full potential. She used her platform to speak out against the status quo, to challenge the idea that women's sports were somehow secondary to their male counterparts. Her participation in this fight was not confined to soundbites or media moments; it was embedded in her everyday actions. Whether through her social media presence, public appearances, or candid interviews, Candace was a force that could not be ignored. She refused to accept the limitations placed on her by a culture that seemed uninterested in supporting women athletes. Instead, Candace led by example, showing that to be a woman in sports was to be resilient, to be unapologetic, and to be willing to fight not just for personal success but for the success of the entire league.

Her impact went beyond the numbers and the wins, though there were plenty of those. Candace's leadership in the WNBA was about building a culture of respect, support, and visibility. She believed deeply that the future of women's basketball was bound not only by talent but by the collective strength of the athletes who made up the league. Candace was a connector. She understood the importance of mentorship and guidance, and she dedicated herself to uplifting younger players, showing them the ropes and guiding them through the intricacies of professional sports, both the triumphs and the frustrations.

Her tenure with the Los Angeles Sparks and later with the Chicago Sky was not just about playing basketball—it was about building a community. Candace became a mentor to the younger generation of WNBA stars, offering advice, sharing her experiences, and leading by example. Her leadership transcended the confines of the court and seeped into every facet of her relationships with her teammates. She understood that to elevate the sport, to truly push the league forward, it wasn't enough to simply be great. One had to lift others with them, sharing knowledge, fostering an environment of collaboration, and demanding excellence from everyone involved.

Candace Parker also brought a distinct visibility to the WNBA, elevating its stature in the public consciousness. Her media presence, amplified by her personality and her knack for connecting with people, became one of the league's most valuable assets. Candace was not just a basketball player; she was a recognizable figure, one who crossed over into mainstream media. She became the face of women's sports, appearing on television, in advertisements, and on the cover of major magazines. Her presence in these spaces was revolutionary, as it opened doors for more female athletes to enter the public sphere in ways they had never been able to before. Candace was not just breaking barriers for herself; she was ensuring that future generations of women would not have to fight as hard for the attention and respect that was rightfully theirs.

Her move to the Chicago Sky in 2021 was another defining moment in her career—one that would prove pivotal not just for her legacy but for the future of the WNBA. Candace's decision to join the Sky, a team that had yet to capture a championship, was both strategic and symbolic. It was clear that she was not just joining a team to add to her trophy case; she was joining a movement, a new wave of talent and leadership that had the potential to change the trajectory of the franchise and, by extension, the league. Her impact in Chicago was felt immediately, as her leadership helped propel the Sky to their first-ever WNBA championship in 2021. The significance of this victory could not be overstated—Candace, with her experience, wisdom, and drive, had not only led a team to victory but had set a new standard for excellence in the WNBA.

Candace Parker's influence on the WNBA will continue to be felt for generations. She was, and is, a trailblazer—someone who not only played the game at the highest level but who also fought to make the game better, more visible, and more equitable for those who would follow. Her legacy is not just in the championships she won, the MVPs she earned, or the records she shattered. Her legacy is in the culture she helped create, the doors she opened, and the future she shaped. Candace Parker didn't just elevate women's sports; she transformed them, making the impossible seem inevitable and ensuring that the WNBA, as well as women's sports more broadly, would never be the same again.

Chapter 11:
Personal Life
Love, Loss, and the Balance of It All

Candace Parker's life off the basketball court was as layered, nuanced, and complex as her career. Behind the public persona of the basketball legend—whose name was synonymous with greatness in the sport—was a woman deeply invested in her personal life, relationships, and the delicate balance of it all. While her legacy as one of the greatest athletes to ever play the game is undeniable, it is the story of love, loss, and personal growth that adds depth to her journey—a story that speaks not only to her resilience on the court but to her vulnerability and humanity off it. As much as Candace's life was defined by her incredible feats in the world of sports, it was also profoundly shaped by the private moments that made her who she truly was.

The journey of balancing the high demands of a professional career with the complexities of personal life is something few athletes, especially women, can ever fully escape. For Candace, the journey was one of constant tension between the athlete and the woman, between the public figure and the private individual. On the court, she was expected to be flawless, to push herself to the absolute limit, to carry not only her team but the hopes and aspirations of a league. Off the court, though, she was simply a woman—someone who loved, who grieved, and who sought a semblance of normalcy in a world that often placed her in a spotlight too bright for anyone to truly handle. Navigating this duality would prove to be both her greatest challenge and her greatest triumph.

From the beginning, Candace was not just a player on the basketball court but a daughter, a sister, and a friend. She grew up in a family where athleticism was revered, where both her parents, Larry and Sara Parker, encouraged her to pursue excellence, yet also emphasized the importance of values, hard work, and perseverance. Candace's father, in particular, was a profound influence on her life. He was both a mentor and a sounding board, offering her wisdom and guidance that shaped her into the person she would become. While basketball was always a family affair, it was her parents' steadfast love and dedication to her success beyond sports that laid the foundation for Candace's belief in herself.

Her relationships with her family would remain an anchor throughout her career. When Candace faced adversity—whether it be an injury, a difficult loss, or a challenging season—she would turn to her family for solace and strength. Through it all, they remained a constant source of support, providing a refuge from the public's ever-watchful gaze. Yet, even within the loving embrace of her family, Candace was not immune to the pain of loss. As with any human being, tragedy and hardship would strike, leaving indelible marks on her soul. And it was through these difficult moments, when her world seemed to fracture, that Candace would demonstrate the quiet resilience that would come to define her off the court.

The loss of her father, Larry Parker, was one of the most significant and painful moments in Candace's life. Larry had been her rock, her guiding light, the person who believed in her even when she doubted herself. His passing was not just the loss of a father; it was the loss of a cornerstone of her identity. The man who had coached her through every challenge, who had celebrated her triumphs and offered counsel through her struggles, was no longer there to share in the milestones of her life. The grief she felt was profound, an ache that transcended the physical and emotional exhaustion that often accompanies such a loss. In the wake of his passing, Candace was forced to confront not only the loss of a loved one but the overwhelming sense of vulnerability that comes when the foundation of your life is shaken. For the first time, she felt truly alone.

Yet, as Candace had done throughout her life, she leaned into the pain and found strength in it. She was no stranger to hardship; she had been tested time and time again on the court and off. And in her grief, she realized that her father's influence, his belief in her, was not something that died with him. It was something she carried within herself—a legacy that would live on in every decision she made, every step she took forward. Candace had always approached her career with an incredible sense of purpose, but after her father's death, that purpose became clearer. She was playing not just for herself, but for him, for everything he had sacrificed, and for the lessons he had taught her about perseverance and resilience.

Candace's personal life was further complicated by the delicate balance of her career and her role as a mother. Becoming a mother was both a joy and a challenge—an experience that would force her to confront the realities of being a professional athlete and a parent. The demands of travel, training, and playing at the highest level left her with limited time to spend with her daughter. Yet, she navigated the complexities of motherhood with the same grace and determination that she applied to every other aspect of her life. Balancing the demands of a professional basketball career with raising a child was no easy task, but Candace's ability to manage both worlds was a testament to her strength, resilience, and love for her family.

Her role as a mother became the grounding force that kept Candace tethered to her true self. The love she felt for her daughter was immeasurable, and it became her motivation to strive for more, not just as an athlete but as a person. Candace wanted to be a role model, not only in her professional achievements but in the way she balanced her personal life, the way she showed her daughter that a woman could do anything, even in the face of obstacles that seemed insurmountable. She did not want her child to see a woman who sacrificed everything for success, but rather one who could have it all—career, family, love, and purpose.

And yet, despite the immense love she had for her family, Candace was also deeply aware of the sacrifices that came with the demands of her career. The time spent away from her family, the constant pressure to perform at the highest level, the scrutiny of her every move—it all added up. It was a tension that many professional athletes, especially women, grapple with throughout their careers. For Candace, the battle to maintain this balance was a constant one. There were moments of guilt, moments when she felt that she was not giving enough to her family or her child. But there were also moments of joy, when she saw her daughter's face light up after a big win, or when her family could share in the triumphs and challenges of her career.

Love, in Candace's life, was not just about her immediate family—it was also about the love she shared with her teammates. Over the years, Candace built deep, lasting friendships with the women she played alongside, relationships that went far beyond the game itself. Basketball had brought them together, but it was the bonds they formed off the court that truly defined their connection. The shared experiences, the late-night talks, the moments of vulnerability—these were the relationships that sustained her throughout her career. These were the women who saw her not just as an athlete, but as a person. They were her sisters in arms, her support system, her closest confidantes.

Despite the external pressures that came with her fame, Candace's personal life was marked by moments of quiet joy, peace, and reflection. The balance of love, loss, and family was not always easy to strike, but it was in these very moments that Candace found the true essence of her journey. The sacrifices, the challenges, the pain of loss—these were the things that shaped her, that gave her the depth and resilience that allowed her to rise time and time again. Through it all, Candace Parker remained grounded, finding strength in the love of those closest to her, in the memory of her father, and in the joy of being a mother. And it was in this balance, this delicate dance between career, love, and family, that Candace Parker truly became the woman she is today—strong, resilient, and unapologetically herself.

Chapter 12:
More Than an Athlete
Identity, Purpose, and Power

There are stories etched on scoreboards, and then there are stories etched on souls—tales not of trophies, but of transformation. The kind that exists in the quiet spaces between fame and fulfillment, where legacy is less about what is seen and more about what is deeply felt. Candace Parker's life belongs to the latter. Her victories on the hardwood are legendary, but her deeper triumph lies in how she redefined what it means to be powerful—not just in athleticism, but in identity, voice, and purpose. She was never content to be merely celebrated for her height, her statistics, or her three-point stroke. She wanted, and dared, to be seen in her entirety.

As the bright lights of packed arenas dimmed and the crowd's roar faded into the silence of self-reflection, Candace stood alone with questions that fame never answers: Who am I beyond the uniform? What legacy do I want to leave that isn't quantified by rings or accolades? Her journey toward these answers became her most important game—one without a clock, but full of consequences.

From the earliest years of her public life, the media attempted to sculpt a pristine image of Candace Parker: the phenom, the prodigy, the once-in-a-generation athlete. She fit neatly into the expectations of fans, networks, and brands—fierce but friendly, competitive but composed. Yet behind every highlight reel was a human being navigating the same labyrinth of selfhood that so many others do, only with the weight of millions of eyes watching.

In those eyes, Candace often played many roles: the girl next door with a sky-high vertical leap, the mother with unmatched grace, the role model with no room for imperfection. But roles, no matter how beloved, can become cages. And eventually, Candace had to ask herself: Was she living for applause or authenticity?

The answer arrived slowly, not in a single moment, but as a quiet uprising in her soul. It grew louder each time she chose honesty over expectation, vulnerability over veneer. The athlete who once soared above defenders with ease found even greater elevation when she began telling her truth, not the carefully edited version fit for press conferences, but the kind that lives in late-night conversations, private journals, and trembling confessions.

When Candace publicly shared her marriage to Anna Petrakova and announced the expansion of their family, it was more than a social media post. It was a declaration of humanity. A statement that greatness isn't diluted by complexity; it's defined by it. In doing so, she shattered the invisible barriers that still linger in professional sports, particularly for women and LGBTQ+ athletes who've long been taught to separate personal identity from professional performance.

Candace didn't just refuse to be placed in a box—she lit the box on fire and built something beautiful in its ashes. Her courage gave language to countless others who had lived in the shadows, and her presence in the spotlight was no longer just about basketball—it became about what was possible when you live in your truth without apology.

The impact of that decision rippled far beyond the court. Brands began to see her not just as an ambassador of sports but as a symbol of integrity. Young girls saw themselves in her not just because she could dunk, but because she dared to live freely. Men, women, boys, girls, queer youth, and everyone in between suddenly saw in Candace the permission to be both exceptional and authentic. She was no longer just a model athlete—she was a mirror, reflecting the complex, messy, beautiful reality of what it means to be whole.

But this kind of freedom isn't won without resistance. With candor came criticism. With transparency came scrutiny. Some fans were uncomfortable. Some sponsors wavered. Some questioned her priorities, as though a person's truth could be separated from their professional value. Through it all, Candace remained unmoved—not unfeeling, but unshaken. Her roots ran deeper than any headline could reach.

She knew that being a leader wasn't about being perfect—it was about being real. And so, she spoke. At panels. In interviews. In classrooms. On television. On court and off it. With every word, she shifted the conversation. Her voice, once reserved for post-game breakdowns, became a symphony of empowerment, identity, justice, and joy.

Candace's influence began to eclipse the boundaries of basketball. She appeared in documentaries that celebrated the lived experiences of Black women. She partnered with brands not just for commercial campaigns, but for cause-based initiatives. She used her platform to advocate for equality in sports, mental health awareness, racial justice, and gender representation. She made it clear: excellence should never cost you your authenticity.

Candace Parker: "Power, Purpose, and the Making of a Legend"

In locker rooms and production studios alike, she created spaces where stories like hers—and unlike hers—could be told without fear. She amplified the voices of those still finding their footing, still gathering the courage to be seen. Every assist she made on the court became a metaphor for the ones she made off of it—lifting others, spotlighting them, reminding them they mattered.

There's a kind of strength that lives in muscle and reflex. It wins games. But there's another kind that lives in honesty and intention. That kind changes culture. Candace wielded both. Her power was never just in her vertical leap or her MVP trophies—it was in her ability to challenge the narrative. To redefine greatness. To invite others into a broader, braver idea of what leadership looks like.

She became not only a North Star for aspiring athletes but also a lighthouse for anyone who ever felt they had to hide parts of themselves to be accepted. And as the years passed, her influence deepened. She wasn't trending—she was transforming. Not a fleeting name in the headlines, but an enduring voice in the heartbeats of movements.

Legacy, Candace knew, isn't about being remembered. It's about helping others remember themselves. And so she poured her energy into purpose-driven work—youth empowerment, inclusive storytelling, and equity in sports. Her business moves were thoughtful, her public stances deliberate. Every project she touched bore the fingerprint of her values.

Behind the camera, she co-produced features that spotlighted underrepresented communities. In front of it, she brought a nuanced, informed perspective to basketball commentary, offering insights that elevated how the women's game was understood and respected. She walked into spaces historically reserved for men and didn't ask for a seat—she brought her own.

There was a poetic symmetry in how she balanced it all: motherhood and media, advocacy and athletics, ambition and authenticity. She wasn't trying to have it all—she was building something bigger than herself. A new model. A new standard. A new language for success.

As Candace Parker entered the twilight of her playing career, the applause never stopped. But it changed. It wasn't just for her stat line—it was for her stance. Her courage. Her consistency. She became the rare kind of icon whose story doesn't fade when the final buzzer sounds. Instead, it reverberates, passed on from generation to generation.

For every young athlete lacing up their sneakers, for every parent teaching their child to believe in who they are, for every person standing at the edge of self-discovery wondering if they're enough, Candace Parker's story whispers a resounding yes. Yes, you can be brilliant and broken. Fierce and fragile. Competitive and compassionate. Yes, you can take up space. Yes, you can speak your truth and still be loved, respected, and revered.

She never asked to be a symbol. But she earned that mantle by living with unwavering alignment between her values and her voice. Her legacy is not a brand—it's a beacon. And the light it casts reminds us all: greatness begins the moment you stop performing and start becoming.

More than an athlete. That's not just a title—it's a tribute. To the woman who played the game like poetry and lived her life like a revolution.

Conclusion
The Lasting Legacy of Candace Parker

Candace Parker's legacy extends far beyond the confines of a basketball court. It is a legacy of resilience, of breaking barriers, of challenging the status quo, and of inspiring generations of women and young athletes to dream bigger and reach higher. Throughout her illustrious career, she embodied the very spirit of what it means to be a champion—not just in terms of titles and accolades, but in the way she carried herself, in her unwavering commitment to improving the game, and in her desire to leave the world better than she found it. Candace Parker is more than just an athlete; she is a symbol of what is possible when you combine talent with heart, passion with perseverance, and ambition with humility.

As the first overall pick in the 2008 WNBA Draft, Candace Parker arrived at the professional level with the weight of great expectations. She was, after all, more than just another talented player; she was the embodiment of hope for women's basketball and the WNBA, a league still fighting for recognition and respect in a world dominated by male athletes. From the very beginning, Candace was not just playing the game of basketball—she was transforming it. Her on-court dominance was undeniable, as she quickly established herself as one of the most skilled and intelligent players the WNBA had ever seen. But Candace's impact was never confined to the hardwood. Her influence stretched far beyond the game, into the hearts and minds of fans, other athletes, and those who saw in her a reflection of their dreams.

Candace's remarkable career was one defined by excellence. She was a two-time MVP, a seven-time WNBA All-Star, a gold medalist with Team USA, and a champion with the Los Angeles Sparks and the Chicago Sky. Each of these accolades represents not just her brilliance but her ability to elevate her teams and the league itself. Every victory she earned, every record she shattered, was a testament to the dedication, work ethic, and mental toughness that defined her as a player. Yet, it wasn't just her skill on the court that made her a legend; it was the way she carried herself, the way she led by example, and the way she brought people together to achieve something greater than any individual accomplishment.

Candace was more than a basketball player—she was a trailblazer for women in sports. She became the face of the WNBA, a role model for young girls everywhere who saw in her not just a great athlete, but a powerful force of change. Her fight for pay equity, better media coverage, and recognition for female athletes was relentless and personal. She used her platform, her voice, and her position as one of the most recognizable figures in sports to demand more for herself and for every other woman who dreamed of playing at the highest level. Candace understood that her success wasn't just about her; it was about the future of the game, the future of women's basketball, and the future of women in sports. She became a symbol of strength and perseverance, not only for what she accomplished in the game but for the battles she fought off the court.

Throughout her career, Candace was also a mentor to younger players, teaching them not only the fundamentals of basketball but also the value of integrity, work ethic, and leadership. She never saw her success as something to be hoarded but rather as something to be shared. Her willingness to guide and support the next generation of athletes was one of the defining features of her legacy. She knew that true greatness was not measured by how many championships you win or how many accolades you collect, but by the positive impact you have on those around you, by the way you inspire others to reach their fullest potential.

The impact of Candace's legacy will continue to be felt long after she steps away from the game. She has laid the groundwork for future generations of athletes, not just in basketball, but in every sport where women have been denied the attention and respect they deserve. Candace's influence extends far beyond the WNBA. She is a role model for young girls in every corner of the globe, showing them that with hard work, dedication, and an unwavering belief in themselves, they can achieve anything. She is proof that the dreams of young girls who want to play sports at the highest level are not only valid but worth fighting for.

As Candace navigates her life after basketball, her influence will continue to resonate. Her transition from athlete to broadcaster, business leader, and advocate for women's rights is a natural evolution of the impact she has had on the world. Candace has already shown that she is more than capable of excelling in every endeavor she undertakes. Her work with Adidas, her role in broadcasting, and her continued advocacy for gender equality are just the beginning of what will undoubtedly be another remarkable chapter in her life. Candace's story will not be confined to the past; it will continue to inspire and shape the future.

Candace Parker's lasting legacy is not just one of championships and accolades, but one of profound cultural change. She has shown us what it means to be a true leader—not just in sports, but in life. Her influence will be felt for generations to come, not just by those who watched her play, but by those who will never know a world without the trail she blazed. Candace Parker has proven that greatness is not about being the best on the court, but about using your platform to create opportunities, to break barriers, and to inspire others to dream big.

In the end, Candace Parker's legacy will be remembered for much more than the statistics or the titles. It will be remembered for the way she elevated the WNBA, for the way she fought for equality, for the way she embodied what it means to be a woman in sports, and for the way she inspired millions to believe in their potential. Her legacy will endure as a symbol of perseverance, resilience, and leadership, a testament to the power of sport to change lives and to the indomitable spirit of a woman who dared to break every barrier placed in her path. Candace Parker's journey may have begun on the basketball court, but her impact will echo far beyond it, shaping the future of women's sports for years to come.

Candace Parker: "Power, Purpose, and the Making of a Legend"

Made in United States
Troutdale, OR
06/02/2025